639.7
LOM
J

W9-BWW-949
Caring for Your Spider

WITHDRAWN

This item was purchased with funds donated by:

A. Sturm & Sons Foundation, Inc.

Caring for Your
Spider

3 1389 01613 9008

Michelle Lomberg

Weigl Publishers Inc.

Project Coordinator
Heather C. Hudak

Design and Layout
Warren Clark
Katherine Phillips

Copy Editor
Jennifer Nault

Photo Research
Tracey Carruthers

Locate the spider webs throughout the book to find useful tips on caring for your pet.

Published by Weigl Publishers Inc.
350 5th Avenue, Suite 3304, PMB 6G
New York, NY 10118-0069 USA
Web site: www.weigl.com

Copyright 2004 WEIGL PUBLISHERS INC.
All rights reserved. No part of this publication may be reproduced, stored in a retrieval system, or transmitted in any form or by any means, electronic, mechanical, photocopying, recording, or otherwise, without the prior written permission of the publisher.

Library of Congress Cataloging-in-Publication Data

Lomberg, Michelle.
  Caring for your spider / Michelle Lomberg.
     v. cm. -- (Caring for your pet)
Contents: Eight-legged friends -- Pet profiles -- Spider history -- Life cycle -- Picking your pet -- Spider supplies -- Feeding a spider -- Spider parts -- Handling your spider -- Healthy and happy -- Spider behavior -- Spider stories -- Pet puzzlers -- Frequently asked questions -- More information.
  ISBN 1-59036-120-2 (Library Bound : alk. paper)
 1. Spiders as pets--Juvenile literature. [1. Spiders as pets. 2. Pets.] I. Title. II. Caring for your pet (Mankato, Minn.)
  SF459.S64L65 2004
  639.7--dc21

                    2003001387

            Printed in the United States of America
            1 2 3 4 5 6 7 8 9 0   07 06 05 04 03

Photograph and Text Credits
Every reasonable effort has been made to trace ownership and to obtain permission to reprint copyright material. The publishers would be pleased to have any errors or omissions brought to their attention so that they may be corrected in subsequent printings.

Cover: Mexican flameknee tarantula (Rick C. West); **Corel Corporation**: pages 5, 16; **Heather Hudak**: page 12; **Photofest**: pages 26, 27; **PhotoSpin, Inc.**: 9; **Dave Taylor**: pages 3, 7 right; **Rick C. West**: title page, pages 4, 6 left, 6 middle, 6 right, 7 left, 7 middle, 8, 10 top, 10 bottom, 11 top, 11 bottom, 13, 14, 15, 17 left, 17 right, 18/19, 20, 21, 22, 23 top, 23 bottom, 24, 25 top, 25 bottom, 28, 30, 31

Contents

Trustworthy 7/04

Eight-legged Friends

All spiders have fangs that eject **venom**. Not all venom is dangerous to humans.

Spiders have a bad reputation. Many people are terrified of these eight-legged creatures, but the truth is that very few spiders are dangerous to humans. Most spiders are shy, gentle creatures that make interesting, unusual pets. Pet spiders are very easy to care for. They are able to live in a small space. They do not need to be brushed or walked, and they do not need to be fed daily.

Most spiders are harmless if they are treated with respect.

Even though spiders do not need much attention, they are still a big responsibility. A spider's enclosure must be kept at the right temperature and **humidity**. It must also be kept clean. Spiders need to eat live food such as crickets and moths. Spiders also require care if they are sick or injured.

Spiders are not like cats or dogs. They spend most of the day hiding and should not be handled often. Spider owners must be very patient. Patience will be rewarded with a glimpse into the lives of these unusual creatures.

▬ Spider webs are very strong. They do not tear when insects fly into them.

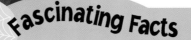

Fascinating Facts

- There are more than 35,000 **species** of spiders.
- The fear of spiders is called *arachnophobia*.
- All spiders make silk, but not all spiders spin webs.
- The largest spider is the goliath bird eater tarantula. His leg span can reach 10 inches in **diameter**.

Pet Profiles

Spiders come in many sizes, colors, and **temperaments**. Most spiders are calm, gentle, and shy. Others are aggressive and may give a painful bite. Only experienced spider owners should keep aggressive or dangerous spiders as pets. Spiders should not be handled often.

MEXICAN REDKNEE TARANTULA

- Black in color with orange bands on leg joints
- Grows to about 5 inches across
- Females can live up to 20 years
- Calm temperament
- Lives in a range of temperatures
- Terrestrial

PINKTOE TARANTULA

- Dark in color with pink or red patches on the ends of its legs
- Females can live 8 or 9 years
- Calm temperament, but can be easily startled
- Spends most of her time hiding in her web
- Arboreal

CHILEAN ROSE TARANTULA

- Tan, pink, or red in color
- Grows to about 4 inches across
- Calm temperament, but may bite if handled
- One of the most common breeds for new spider owners to raise
- Terrestrial

Tarantulas are the largest spiders. They are also the most common pet spiders. There are more than 800 species of tarantula.

Other spiders kept as pets include giant orb weavers, widows, and wolf spiders. Common house and garden spiders can also make enjoyable pets.

Most spiders are either terrestrial or arboreal. Terrestrial spiders live in burrows in the ground. Arboreal spiders live in trees.

CAROLINA WOLF SPIDER

- Gray-brown in color with gray hair
- Adult females grow to 4 inches across
- Females can live 3 years; males live 1.5 years
- Should not be handled
- Requires little care
- Terrestrial

FALSE WIDOW SPIDER

- Dark in color with yellow, white, or red markings
- Smaller than 1 inch across
- Weak venom makes them less dangerous than the black widow spider
- Calm temperament
- Requires little care
- Arboreal

GOLDEN SILK ORB WEAVER

- Gray-brown in color with golden brown markings
- Grows to 5 inches across
- Weaves large, golden webs
- Calm temperament
- Needs a large living space
- Arboreal

Spider History

Spiders have lived on Earth for about 400 million years. This history has been difficult to study because spider **fossils** are difficult to find. Spider fossils are rare because spiders have soft bodies with no bones. A few ancient spiders have been preserved in **amber**. Others have left impressions in soft rock. Using this information, scientists have been able to trace the history of spiders.

Spiders are *Arthropods*. *Arthropod* is a Greek word that means "jointed feet." Insects and shellfish, such as crabs and lobsters, are *Arthropods*, too. *Arthropods* are descendants of ancient worms called *Annelida*. These were similar to modern earthworms.

In the U.S., fewer than five people die from spider bites each year.

House spiders, such as the giant house spider, are commonly found in closets, basements, garages, and dark spaces.

Spiders belong to a special class of *Arthropods* that are called *Arachnids*. The *Arachnid* group also includes mites, ticks, and scorpions. The very first *Arachnids* lived in the water about 450 million years ago. They looked like scorpions. The earliest land *Arachnids* were *Trigonotarbids*, or trigs. Trigs looked like tiny spiders, but they did not have fangs or **spinnerets**.

The first modern spider lived about 380 million years ago. Even though spiders have lived with humans for thousands of years, it was not until the 1970s that they became popular pets.

The earliest scorpion fossils date back about 420 million years. This is about 200 years before dinosaurs roamed Earth.

Fascinating Facts

- Spider webs have been used as folk remedies to cure warts and to stop bleeding.
- The nursery rhyme character Little Miss Muffet was a real girl. Her father believed that eating spiders would cure the common cold.
- Spiders have no bones.
- There are about 35,000 spider species. About 3,000 species live in North America.

Life Cycle

The life span of spiders depends on the species. Many smaller spiders live only 1 year. Some tarantulas live more than 20 years. In all species, females live longer than males.

Eggs

Spiders begin life as eggs. The female spider spins a special web called an egg sac to hold her eggs. Some spiders carry the sac with them, and others hide it. Eggs take a few weeks to a few months to hatch, depending on the species and the temperature.

Mature Spiders

Spiders have soft bodies that are covered in a hard exoskeleton. The exoskeleton is an outer skin that cannot grow. Spiders must shed the exoskeleton when they have outgrown it. This process is called molting. Most spiders molt once in a while until they are adults. Mature female tarantulas continue to molt once or twice each year.

Fascinating Facts

- Some spiders lay only a few eggs. Others lay as many as 2,000.
- The eggs of some large spiders are the size of green peas.
- Some tarantulas can take as long as 10 years to mature.

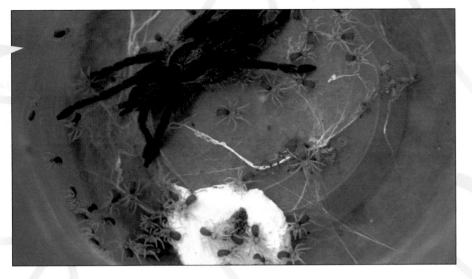

Hatchlings

Most hatchlings are born hairless, colorless, and without claws. They cannot eat. Hatchlings remain in the egg sac until they shed their outer skin and grow a new one.

Spiderlings

Once spiderlings have shed their first skin, they begin to eat. Their first meal is usually an unhatched egg or a weaker sibling. Most spiderlings must fend for themselves. For some species, the mother cares for her babies. She protects them and brings them food until they are able to look after themselves. The wolf spider carries her babies on her back until they are 1 week old. Other spiderlings spin a strand of silk that allows them to be carried off by the wind.

Picking Your Pet

If you think you need to be fearless to own a spider, think again. Spiders are timid, fragile animals. They need an owner who will be patient and gentle. Consider the following questions before choosing your pet.

What Will a Spider Cost?

The best place to buy a spider is from a **reputable** pet store or **breeder**. The cost of your spider will depend on the species. Rare spiders are more expensive. When calculating the cost of buying a pet spider, be sure to include the cost of food, an enclosure, and supplies. Spiders need to eat live food such as crickets, mealworms, or baby mice. Spiders do not need to make regular visits to a **veterinarian**. They rarely require medical treatment, and they do not need to be **vaccinated**.

▬ The rose hair tarantula has a calm temperament and makes a good pet.

Fascinating Facts

- The Australian funnel web spider can pierce bone with its fangs.
- No two spider webs are the same.
- The female golden silk orb weaver is about 1 inch across. The male golden silk orb weaver is only one-eighth of an inch across.

How Should I Choose My Spider?

Choose a spider that has been bred in **captivity**. Spiders captured in nature are in danger of one-day becoming **extinct**.

How Will Owning a Spider Affect My Family?

Many people are afraid of spiders. Before bringing a spider home, find out if members of your family are afraid of them. Try to educate your family about spiders using books, television programs, videos, and Web sites. If the thought of sharing a home with a spider still scares family members, you should consider a different pet.

If any member of your household has a history of allergies, you should not get a spider. Very few spiders have venom that can kill a person. However, even weak venom can cause an allergic reaction. Even if you are not allergic to spiders, tarantula hairs can produce a terrible rash.

Always keep your spider's cage at the proper humidity. If your spider's exoskeleton becomes too dry, he may have trouble molting.

Some captive spiders throw off **urticating** hairs when they are scared or stressed.

Spider Supplies

Your spider will need to live in an enclosure. The type of enclosure depends on the type of spider. Is he terrestrial or arboreal? Does he thrive in a dry or humid climate? Learn as much as you can about your spider in order to provide the most suitable enclosure.

Most spiders should live alone. If two or more spiders are housed together, they may kill and eat each other. Your spider's enclosure should be about twice as wide as his leg span, and about three times as long. If you have a burrowing spider, the top of the enclosure should not be too high. Falling from a height of just 6 inches can kill a spider. Arboreal spiders need larger, taller enclosures than terrestrial spiders.

If your spider's enclosure is too dry, use a spray bottle to sprinkle a fine mist. Do not spray the spider directly.

■ Be sure that your tarantula's enclosure has a secure lid because most can climb very well.

Some tarantulas, such as the Peruvian pinktoe, use their large size and strength to catch small frogs and lizards.

Plastic boxes with snap-on lids are ideal for terrestrial spiders. Be sure to punch several small holes into the lid to let air in. Glass fish tanks can also make a suitable home for some spiders. The tank should have a secure lid.

The spider's enclosure will need a **substrate**. For burrowing spiders, this should be a mixture of sand, peat moss, bark chips, and vermiculite, or minerals that absorb water. The type of mixture depends on how much humidity your spider needs. Pine and cedar bark are **toxic** to spiders and should not be used. Arboreal spiders will need some branches on which to build their web.

If you remove food **carcasses** regularly, you should only have to clean out your spider's enclosure twice a year. Use a long pair of tweezers to remove food carcasses.

Fascinating Facts

- Some spiders are communal, which means they live in large groups. A communal web can hold as many as 20,000 spiders.
- Water spiders live underwater. They build bell-shaped webs and fill them with air bubbles.

Feeding Your Spider

All spiders are carnivores. This means they are meat-eaters. Most spiders eat insects. Some large tarantulas eat mice, lizards, and other small animals. Not all spiders use their webs to catch food. Some lie in wait for their **prey**. Others chase their meal. All spiders use their venom to stun or kill their prey.

Since spiders do not have teeth for chewing, they are only able to drink their food. Spiders inject their prey with digestive juices. These juices turn the prey's insides into liquid. The spider sucks this liquid and leaves the carcass behind.

Most spiders will only eat live food. Crickets are the most common food for pet spiders.

If you catch insects or worms to feed your spider, be sure they have not been sprayed with **pesticides**.

■ Spiders may stop eating for a few weeks before they molt.

Live crickets can be purchased at a pet store. Beetles, earthworms, grasshoppers, houseflies, and moths are also good food for a spider.

It is important to remove uneaten food and carcasses from your spider's enclosure. Live prey can produce young that may attack your spider while it is molting. Leftover carcasses can grow fungus or attract **parasites** that are dangerous to your spider.

Spiders need fresh water. Provide clean water in a shallow dish. Place a piece of sponge inside the water dish. If your spider falls in the water, she can climb out using the sponge. Replace the sponge regularly so that it does not grow mold.

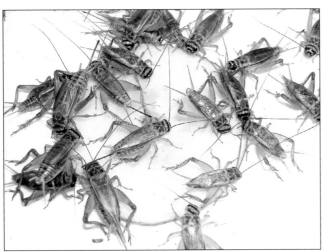
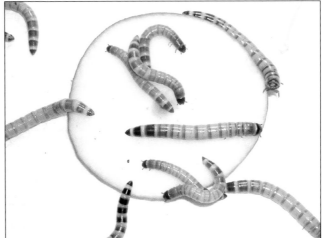

Buying crickets and mealworms from a pet store can be quite costly. You may want to raise your own.

Fascinating Facts

- It takes a tarantula 1 to 2 days to digest a mouse.
- The bola spider throws a sticky ball of silk at her prey.

Spider Parts

With their hard exoskeletons and quick movements, spiders have much in common with ants and beetles. However, spiders are not insects. There are several differences between spiders and insects. Insects have six legs and three main body parts. Spiders have eight legs and two main body parts.

The spider's back end is called the abdomen. The abdomen is the most fragile part of a spider.

A spider's silk comes out of his spinnerets. Spiders spin different kinds of silk for different purposes.

Spiders hear through slits in the exoskeleton. Most of these slits are near the leg joints. Each slit has a thin **membrane** like an eardrum. This membrane senses vibrations.

A spider breathes through slits in his abdomen. His lungs are called book lungs because they look like the pages of a book. Book lungs are not very efficient. A spider cannot run far before he must stop to catch his breath.

All spiders have eight legs. Spiders taste and smell through organs in their legs.

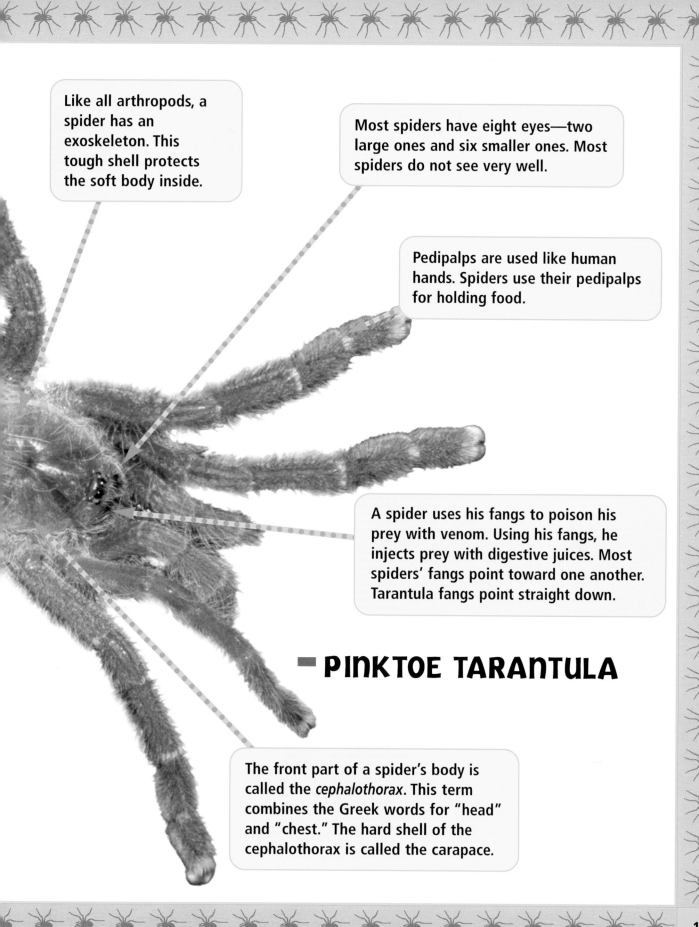

Like all arthropods, a spider has an exoskeleton. This tough shell protects the soft body inside.

Most spiders have eight eyes—two large ones and six smaller ones. Most spiders do not see very well.

Pedipalps are used like human hands. Spiders use their pedipalps for holding food.

A spider uses his fangs to poison his prey with venom. Using his fangs, he injects prey with digestive juices. Most spiders' fangs point toward one another. Tarantula fangs point straight down.

PINKTOE TARANTULA

The front part of a spider's body is called the *cephalothorax*. This term combines the Greek words for "head" and "chest." The hard shell of the cephalothorax is called the carapace.

Handling Your Spider

Handling a spider is always risky. Spiders do not enjoy being handled. All spiders can bite. A spider's bite can be very harmful to a human. If a spider is accidentally dropped, she can be seriously injured or killed. To prevent your spider from being injured, she should be handled as little as possible.

▬ When handling a spider, keep your hand close to a solid surface.

If you must remove a spider from her enclosure, it is safest to use a container. Place the opening of a jar or plastic container in front of your spider. Using a soft paintbrush, gently nudge the spider toward the container. Once the spider is inside, place the lid on the container. Make sure there are small air holes in the lid.

To prevent injury to your pet, never pick your spider up by her abdomen.

■ Do not force or scoop your spider into a container. This may cause injuries to her legs or abdomen.

Fascinating Facts

- The body of a newly-molted spider is very fragile. She cannot stand or move until her legs have hardened. Never handle a molting spider.
- Tarantulas head for higher ground when startled. They may run up a person's arm if spooked.

Healthy and Happy

Most veterinarians do not treat spiders. Still, a veterinarian who specializes in exotic pets may be able to answer questions about your spider's health.

Two things that can harm a pet spider are injuries and parasites. Spiders can injure their legs if they fall, if they have trouble molting, or if they are attacked by a **predator**. A spider can survive the loss of a leg. Special muscles at the base of the leg close the wound and stop the bleeding. A new leg will grow when the spider molts. An injury to the abdomen is very serious. If the wound is small, it may be sealed with a dab of petroleum jelly.

If your spider looks shriveled and walks awkwardly, he is probably dehydrated. Make sure your spider always has fresh drinking water.

new leg

Young spiders are able to grow new legs. The new leg will grow in size every time the spider molts.

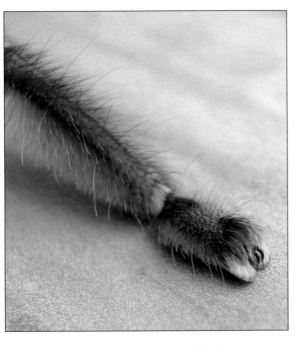

Parasites can threaten the health of your spider. Mites and scuttle flies are the most common pests. Mites are tiny, light-colored dots that might crawl on a spider. Mites can enter a spider's lungs and make him ill. Mites can also attack the spider while he is molting. Scuttle flies lay eggs on tarantulas. When the eggs hatch, the **maggots** crawl into the spider's mouth and eat his insides. Mites and scuttle flies are attracted to the spider's uneaten food. Promptly removing waste from the enclosure can help prevent these pests from harming your spider.

■ Spiders have many types of hair. Some hairs help the spider walk on different surfaces or sense movement. Other hairs prevent the spider from getting stuck in his own web.

■ Some wasps injure spiders and then lay eggs on them. When the eggs hatch, the young wasps feed on the spider.

Fascinating Facts

- Spider blood is blue.
- A spider's heart is shaped like a long tube.

Spider Behavior

A happy spider is usually an inactive spider. Most spiders are content to spend all day in their enclosure. Spiders build different kinds of shelters inside their enclosures. Some terrestrial spiders dig burrows in the substrate. Others hide under pieces of bark or other objects. Arboreal spiders spin shelters out of silk. Most spiders are nocturnal. This means they only leave their shelters at night.

A tarantula bite is said to feel like a bee sting.

Make sure your spider has a place to hide inside his enclosure.

Pet Peeves

Spiders do not like:
- being handled
- other spiders
- too much attention
- bright lights
- loud noises

When threatened, spiders hiss and rear up to make themselves appear bigger.

A spider will let you know when she is stressed or scared. Digging, pacing, or climbing are signs that a spider is not happy in her home. A scared or angry spider will try to look bigger by raising her abdomen. She may rear up and show her fangs. Some species even hiss when they are angry. Many tarantulas brush the hair off their abdomens when they feel threatened. These hairs, called urticating hairs, are a weapon. They can cause skin, eye, and throat irritation. If a spider shows any of these signs, she may be dangerous to handle.

Fascinating Facts

- Some spiders use **camouflage** to hide from their enemies. One species, called the bird-dropping spider, disguises herself as a bird dropping.
- Natural enemies of spiders include birds, frogs, lizards, toads, and wasps.

Spider Stories

In all parts of the world, spiders have fascinated people throughout history. Spiders appear in the mythology of people from ancient Rome, Africa, and North America.

Arachnids are named after Arachne, a character in Roman mythology. Arachne was very proud of her ability to weave. One day, the goddess Minerva challenged Arachne to a weaving contest. Arachne's weaving was better than that of the goddess. Minerva was furious. Arachne felt terrible that she had angered the goddess. She was so upset, she hanged herself. Minerva felt sorry for the girl. Minerva changed Arachne into a spider so Arachne could continue weaving.

■ The book *Charlotte's Web* was made into a film in 1973.

Fascinating Facts

- Perhaps the most popular American spider story is *Charlotte's Web* by E. B. White. This novel tells the story of a clever spider who writes messages in her web to save a pig's life.
- The people of Taranto, Italy, once believed that a spider bite could only be cured by performing a lively dance called the *Tarantella*.

Native Peoples of North America have great respect for spiders. In Hopi mythology, the Spider Woman helped create life on Earth. Using dirt and saliva, she created a pair of twins. One twin formed the new Earth into solid ground. The other gave the world its sounds and echoes.

Today, spiders appear in books and movies. The Spider-Man comic book series was created in the 1960s. The story is about a boy named Peter Parker who becomes a superhero after he is bit by a spider. The comic book was made into a television cartoon series and a movie.

Spider-Man has been the subject of a comic book series and a cartoon. The story of Spider-Man was made into a movie in 2002.

Grandmother Spider Steals the Fire

The Choctaw Peoples of Tennessee and Mississippi believe the Grandmother Spider taught humans how to make and use fire. When people first came to be on Earth, their bodies were wrapped in cocoons. The Great Spirit sent someone to Earth to unwrap them and open their eyes. Since Earth was dark, their eyes saw nothing, and the air was cold. To warm their bodies and light their way, Grandmother Spider left to steal fire from people in the East. When she returned, she taught humans how to use fire. She also taught humans how to make clay pottery and weave.

Pet Puzzlers

What do you know about spiders? If you can answer the following questions correctly, you may be ready to own a pet spider.

Q How can I tell if my spider is angry?

An angry spider might rear up, bare his fangs, and raise his abdomen. Some species hiss when they are angry.

Q Should you decorate your spider's enclosure with pine and cedar bark?

No. Pine and cedar are toxic to spiders.

Q What is the difference between a terrestrial spider and an arboreal spider?

A terrestrial spider lives on the ground. An arboreal spider lives in a tree.

Q Is it a good idea to keep two spiders in the same cage?

It is not a good idea to keep two spiders in the same cage. Sometimes spiders fight or even kill one another.

Q Why should you buy a spider bred in captivity?

Spiders caught in nature are in danger of becoming extinct. Captive breeding helps protect spiders in their natural habitats.

Q Do spiders chew their food?

No. Spiders drink their food. They use digestive juices to turn their prey to liquid.

Q Why do spiders molt?

Spiders molt because their hard exoskeletons cannot grow. When a spider gets too big for his skin, he must molt.

Calling Your Spider

Before you buy your pet spider, write down some spider names that you like. Some names may work better for a female spider. Others may suit a male spider. Here are just a few suggestions:

Hairy

Spinner

Fang

Spidey

Octavia

Boris

Charlotte

Itsy-Bitsy

Webster

Frequently Asked Questions

Should I put toys or decorations in my spider's enclosure?

Spiders do not need to play. If you want to decorate your spider's enclosure, make sure you do not use anything that can fall or roll on top of your spider. House plants make a nice addition to a spider's enclosure. Plants also keep the air humid. Small pots can be secured in the substrate.

If my spider is lying on his back, is he dead?

Spiders lie on their backs to molt. Dead spiders usually lie on their bellies with their legs curled underneath.

Is it legal to own a spider?

Some states have passed laws banning people from keeping certain species of spiders as pets. If you buy your spider from a reputable pet store or breeder, she is probably legal. Still, it is a good idea to check the state and local laws before you buy a spider.

More Information

Animal Organizations

You can help spiders stay healthy and happy by learning more about them. Many organizations are dedicated to teaching people how to care for and protect their pet pals. For more spider information, write to the following organizations:

American Arachnological Society
American Museum of Natural History
Central Park West at 79th Street
New York, NY 10024-5192

American Tarantula Society
P.O. Box 756
Carlsbad, NM 88211-0756

Web Sites

To answer more of your spider questions, go online and surf to the following Web sites:

American Arachnological Society
www.americanarachnology.org

American Tarantula Society
www.atshq.org

Petbugs.com
www.petbugs.com

Words to Know

amber: the hardened sap of ancient trees

breeder: a person who raises specific types of animals or plants

camouflage: special coloring that allows animals to hide

captivity: the state of being kept or owned

carcasses: dead bodies

diameter: the measurement of a straight line passing through the center of a circle

extinct: no longer living anywhere on Earth

fossils: rocklike remains of ancient animals or plants

humidity: moisture

maggots: worms hatched from the eggs of flies

membrane: a thin, skin-like tissue

parasites: animals or plants that feed off another animal or plant

pesticides: chemicals that kill insects and spiders

predator: an animal that hunts for food

prey: an animal that is hunted for food

reputable: known to be honest and fair

species: a group of similar plants or animals

spinnerets: the organs with which a spider spins silk

substrate: the bottom layer of a spider's enclosure

temperaments: personalities

toxic: poisonous

urticating: stinging or irritating; may cause a rash

vaccinated: to protect from a disease

venom: a poisonous liquid some animals use to cause harm to predators and prey

veterinarian: animal doctor

Index